'Children's lives are full of big challenges that adults often don't see. Hearing stories about how other children handle their worries prompts creative solutions and hope. This story of a little girl named Maya and her pet hamster Harry is a story full of those hopeful solutions. We are treated to an adventure in Maya's secret dreamworlds where she discovers how she can tackle her own worries and who she can get help from. She shows us the importance of trust, talking and breathing slowly. I love that award-winning author, Dr Mine Conkbayir has put her knowledge of neuroscience to use in a brand-new way. We could all do with more of the wisdom Maya gains in her dreams. We need more stories like this one – because it boosts insights for children and adults alike.'

—**Suzanne Zeedyk**, trauma specialist, child psychologist and founder of Connected Baby

'Dr Mine Conkbayir's book is an incredible, magical insight into some of the complex emotions many young children and their families can experience when life is a little confusing. There is a purity and honesty of both the storytelling and the characters of Maya and Harry. Their partnership is heartfelt and warm.

You can't help but feel you are on their journey as the story evolves in the different worlds. The impact is quite profound. You start to relate and want to understand and learn more of how children feel in times of trouble, which is very powerful.

You finish the story on a high, with a reality of how sharing our feelings, being kind and talking can only inspire others.

Can't wait for the next chapter!'

—**Paul Adams**, *founder of the charity, Power of Parenting and Public Protection Advisor for the Metropolitan Police*

Maya's ACE Adventures!

Maya knows that her life can be tough sometimes – really tough, but with the help of those she trusts (especially her pet hamster, Harry) Maya discovers her own strength and bravery to overcome the problems she faces.

By day, Maya is a girl who loves drawing and playing football, but she often feels sad and angry when her mum and her boyfriend argue and when she is visiting her dad in prison. By night, Maya is an adventurer – meeting exotic creatures in a kaleidoscopic forest, scuba diving in the ocean and going head-to-head with bullies at a spectacular circus – who faces her fears, helps others and knows just what to do to overcome her problems. As her dreamworlds and real world collide, Maya learns how to conquer life's challenges with the love and support of her family, friends and schoolteacher, Miss Hero.

Beautifully illustrated by Chloe Evans and with a Foreword by Sir Lenny Henry CBE, *Maya's ACE Adventures!* is both a magical adventure for readers of

7+ and a creative tool to foster hope and resilience for children who have survived traumatic experiences.

Dr Mine Conkbayir is an award-winning author, trainer and researcher passionate about bridging the knowledge gap between neuroscience and the early years (EY) sector. A key contributor to the Birth to Five Matters non-statutory guidance for the Early Years Foundation Stage and designer of the first-ever neuroscience-informed qualifications for the EY sector, her latest award-winning book, *Early Childhood and Neuroscience. Theory, Research and Implications for Practice,* is in its second edition and her latest book, *The Neuroscience of the Developing Child. Self-Regulation for Wellbeing and a Sustainable Future* is out now.

Maya's ACE Adventures!
A Story to Celebrate Children's Resilience Following Adverse Childhood Experiences

Written by **Dr Mine Conkbayir**

Illustrated by **Chloe Evans**

With a Foreword by **Sir Lenny Henry CBE**

"Dr Mine Conkbayir's book is heartfelt
and instructional in the best way"
Sir Lenny Henry CBE

Routledge
Taylor & Francis Group
LONDON AND NEW YORK

Designed cover image: Artwork by Chloe Evans

First published 2024
by Routledge
4 Park Square, Milton Park, Abingdon, Oxon OX14 4RN

and by Routledge
605 Third Avenue, New York, NY 10158

Routledge is an imprint of the Taylor & Francis Group, an informa business

British Library Cataloguing-in-Publication Data
A catalogue record for this book is available from the British Library

Library of Congress Cataloging-in-Publication Data
Names: Conkbayir, Mine, author. | Evans, Chloe, illustrator. |
    Henry, Lenny, writer of foreword.
Title: Maya's ace adventures! : a story to celebrate children's resilience
    following adverse childhood experiences / written by Mine Conkbayir ;
    illustrated by Chloe Evans ; with a forward by Lenny Henry, CBE.
Description: Abingdon, Oxon ; New York, NY : Routledge, 2023. | Audience:
    Ages 7-9. | Audience: Grades 2-3. | Summary: A young girl named Maya escapes
    from life's challenges by adventuring into a dreamland at night, but with the
    support of her family, friends, and schoolteacher she discovers her own
    strength to conquer life's challenges.
Identifiers: LCCN 2022061045 (print) | LCCN 2022061046 (ebook) |
    ISBN 9781032368177 (paperback) | ISBN 9781003333944 (ebook)
Subjects: CYAC: Family life—Fiction. | Emotions—Fiction. | Adjustment—
    Fiction. | LCGFT: Picture books.
Classification: LCC PZ7.1.C6459 May 2023 (print) | LCC PZ7.1.C6459 (ebook) |
    DDC [E]—dc23
LC record available at https://lccn.loc.gov/2022061045
LC ebook record available at https://lccn.loc.gov/2022061046

ISBN: 978-1-032-36817-7 (pbk)
ISBN: 978-1-003-33394-4 (ebk)

DOI: 10.4324/b23181

Typeset in Gill Sans MT
by Apex CoVantage, LLC

Printed in the UK by Severn, Gloucester on responsibly sourced paper

This Book is Dedicated to

This storybook, *Maya's ACE Adventures!* is dedicated to all children who have had to overcome many struggles through no fault of their own.

To every one of those children, I say – **you** are a very special and valuable person. You are strong and – you can be whatever you wish to be.

Never let anyone make you think any different.

Lots of love, from Mine.

Foreword

To the reader . . .

Hey you.

Many people think that because you're a comedian, that life is one big roller coaster of laughs and smiles, ice cream and cake and new trainers. It can be for some. But sometimes people can forget that comedians were children too.

I know it sounds hard to believe, but I was Maya's age once. I was bullied at school. I found out I was black at a very early age and that caused name-calling and people hitting me for no reason and all that nonsense. I wish I'd had Maya's *keepers* with me – I might have dealt with those problems in a better way.

Dr Mine Conkbayir's book is heartfelt and instructional in the best way – it's a good story, but is also amusing and has coping tools to help children living in a toxic environment, or coping with an incarcerated parent or being bullied at school. Mine writes about things that affected her as a child and the book handles this subject matter with a light touch. We, as parents get the idea, but any child listening to this story will get an idea (without necessarily having to travel to magical worlds) that these problems can be solved by kindness and self-care.

As I read, I found myself rooting for Maya (and her mum, boyfriend and dad) and wanting her to overcome her obstacles. This book is for any adult seeking some kind of template for communicating with a child who, through no fault of their own, is having to cope with a number of obstacles . . . Problems *can* be overcome Mine's book tells us: with kindness, listening and talisman-like *keepers* that remind us to be kind, talk to each other and to have empathy.

You can't say fairer than that.

Thanks for listening.
Sir Lenny Henry CBE

and with its beak, placed the object in the palm of her hand. She could hardly believe her eyes. "It's a rose-coloured crystal! Crystals have healing powers." "I think that's their way of thanking you for helping them, Maya", responded Harry in his gruff voice. "You were brave and told them that you could help them – you put the egg back in their nest and stopped them arguing."

"Thank you very much!" said Maya to the bird. "I'll always remember you both – and your egg!"

"Let's take it home with us. It might help stop mum and her boyfriend arguing", she said, as she unbuttoned her bag and gently tucked it inside. "I think that's a great idea, Maya!" Harry said. "It could be your *keeper* – a special object to remind you that you are strong and can achieve whatever you want to", as he put his tiny paw on her hand, smiling. "Aaah thanks, Harry. I like that a lot. My very own *keeper*! Now, we'd better go back, it's getting dark!"

Before she knew it, Maya felt her mum's tender arms around her. "Wake up darling, it's time for breakfast". Maya had a big stretch, yawned and jumped up, remembering her dream. She felt in her bag – and yes! the crystal was still there – her special bag brought back the *keeper*. Gripping it tightly, Maya began to feel a warm glow from deep inside her. It made her feel powerful, strong and ready for the day ahead.

Maya gave Harry some breakfast while brushing his beautiful, soft coat. She then went to the bathroom to wash her face before going downstairs to sit at the breakfast table. Her mum and her boyfriend apologised for the night before, explaining that it was not Maya's fault. "I hate it when you argue. Harry doesn't like it either. I have to cover his little ears and tell him it will be alright – every time." Maya's mum looked at her, clearly upset. "It must be horrible, darling. I am very sorry." Looking at her mum, Maya placed the crystal on the breakfast table. "What's this pretty stone?" asked her mother. "It's a pink crystal. It might help you." Maya's mum looked fascinated.

"Thanks Maya! That's very thoughtful of you, darling", she said, and carefully placed it on the mantelpiece.

Maya felt excited because she had football practice after school on Fridays, followed by a trip to her favourite restaurant, with her mum and her mum's boyfriend. Maya's day at school went by without too many problems, although she didn't like having to do the maths test in the morning, especially after hearing all the arguing and objects being smashed the night before. She didn't feel very prepared for the test at all – and 7x6 came up! By the time Maya got home that evening, she was very tired. Her mum prepared Maya's bath before bedtime and made her a lovely hot chocolate to drink after.

As Maya sat on the sofa to drink it, Maya's mum reminded her that they were going to visit her dad tomorrow. Maya begun to feel those butterflies and knots in her tummy again. She fell silent for a few minutes. Her mum could tell that she was upset, so she tried to reassure her. "Daddy will be really happy to see you, sweetheart." Maya continued to sit in silence, with her head down. Without looking up at her mum, she replied "he doesn't care about me". Maya's mum tried to comfort her, but it was no good. She burst into tears and ran up to her room, leaving her unfinished hot chocolate behind. Maya's mum took the hot chocolate and followed her. She knocked on Maya's door. "GO AWAY!" she shouted through her tears. Maya felt very angry – as if a volcano was about to erupt inside her.

Her mum turned the door handle and let herself in. "Your dad loves you very much", she replied, tenderly.

"I don't want to go. Why is he in prison anyway?"
Her mum calmly explained that her dad made some poor choices and had broken the law – which is like

breaking rules – and that when adults break the law, they sometimes have to spend some time in prison, to show they are sorry for what they have done. Maya felt very jumbled up inside. She loved her dad but felt angry at him for being in prison – nor did she want to spend a significant amount of her weekend having to travel far away to see him. She laid down on her bed. Her mum stroked her hair, assuring her that one day, her dad would be free. She kissed Maya on the forehead, wished her and Harry sweet dreams and left the room.

Maya felt very sad – and tired. Her eyes slowly closed and opened and closed again, as she whispered to herself

"Dreams, come tonight – help make it right!"

In no time at all, Maya and Harry found themselves deep in the ocean! Maya felt soothed by the warm water surrounding her and liked watching the patterns created in the water as she moved around. It made her feel calm inside.

Maya looked at Harry and thought he looked brilliant in his miniature scuba diving gear!

But what were they doing here? Maya and Harry swam around, looking at all the stunning sea turtles, starfish and fish among the colourful coral.

After swimming for a long while and counting all the different types of fish they saw on the way, Maya noticed a giant sea turtle caught in an old fishing net, struggling to get free. Maya started to panic and began to breathe very quickly – her heart was pounding in her chest.

"Look, Harry! Poor turtle – it's trapped!"

"Don't panic, Maya. Try to slow your breathing. Watch me and do what I do." Harry took a slow breath in and an even slower deep breath out. Maya copied him. She started to feel calmer. "Thanks, my furry friend! I'll remember that top tip! Hey, I have an idea – your sharp teeth could cut through that net in no time! Give it a go, Harry."

Harry started to nibble at the net, but the net was so enormous and entangled, that his nibbling barely made a difference – they still couldn't reach the turtle and Harry was getting tired. Noticing this, Maya reached into her bag, frantically feeling around for something sharp to help him free the turtle. "Ball of elastic bands. I don't think so. Packet of sweets. Colouring pencils and journal. No. Wait a minute! What's this? My scissors!" Maya grabbed them and started to quickly cut the net as Harry nibbled through it some more. Even with the scissors, it took them some time and a lot of effort to cut through the net, as it was so thick. They also had to make sure that the turtle didn't get hurt from all the cutting, but they persisted and managed to free the turtle.

"WE DID IT!" the terrific two excitedly shouted!

The turtle jubilantly splashed about! She did somersaults and twirls of joy, as if to say "thank you" to them both. Now she was free to swim up to the beach, where she could lay her eggs. As she swam away, Maya noticed two very cool conch shells – a smaller one nestled inside a larger one.

She recognised these beautifully coloured spiral shells from a book she had recently read in class about oceans, remembering that people blow into large conch shells to make a trumpet-like sound to communicate with one another – and they look like snail shells! Maya didn't hesitate to pick them up. "Harry! More *keepers*!" Harry gave her a high-five!

"Maya" . . . "Maya" . . . "wakey-wakey!" Maya's mum was calling her to wake up. With her thoughts still on the tropical ocean, Maya realised

that she and Harry had been on another wonderful, magical dream adventure. And sure enough, when she looked in her bag, there they were – the two conch shells! Maya held these precious *keepers* ever so tightly and she began to feel the same warm glow deep inside her.

She decided to give the larger conch shell to her dad when she visited him on Saturday. That way, they could be connected by whispering a message to each other into their conch shell at the same time, every day.

Maya joined her mum and her boyfriend at the breakfast table. She explained that she had a gift to give to her dad. Her mum said "that's a lovely idea! So kind of you, darling. I know how difficult it is for you to see your dad in prison – and not being able to spend time with him whenever you want to."

The prison was a large and very tall grey building. It looked spooky and scary.

Maya didn't feel so good. She held her mum's hand tightly as they walked through the big black gates. When they reached inside, Maya's mum had to fill in some forms before they both walked through security, one at a time. They had to stand with their arms out – "a bit like an aeroplane" as the friendly prison officer told Maya, which made her laugh and feel a bit less scared. The officer then waved a silver wand around them both, to make sure they were not carrying any prohibited objects.

They were told to take a seat in the waiting room for their names to be called before they could go and see her dad. Maya hadn't seen him for a few months – she felt nervous, shy and angry, even though she did miss him.

It was their time. Maya's dad was standing there waiting for them, clearly excited. "Come here, munchkin!" he said to Maya, with his arms wide open. Maya looked at him, smiling, but continuing to hold her mum's hand tightly. "Go on, darling", her mum said, encouraging her. "It's ok", said her dad. "My munchkin just needs a bit of time." They all sat down around a small table.

"Daddy, I wish you weren't in prison", Maya told him quietly. "I wish I wasn't too, munchkin. I am so sorry. I miss you so much and I think about you all the time." Remembering her *keepers* that she had brought along, Maya suddenly felt happy. "Daddy! I've got something for you!" Maya reached into her pocket and took out the two conch shells. "Well, actually, it's something for both of us. We can send each other a message at the same time every day." Maya's dad looked as if he were about to cry. "That is a brilliant idea" he replied. "Hello, munchkin. It's daddy here!" Maya held her conch to her ear. "Hi daddy, I can hear you!", laughing as she replied. Her dad told Maya "I love you to the moon and back. Never forget that."

By Monday, Maya was feeling a little bit brighter – her mum and her boyfriend hadn't argued last night and she was still feeling the warmth from seeing her dad. Maya skipped into school happily. One of her best friends, Archie, was waiting for her in the playground. "Hey Maya!" They greeted each other in their usual, special way by making a funny face at each other.

They ran inside and headed straight for assembly. Time seemed to go by slowly and Maya found it difficult to sit still for a long time, so it took all her effort to pay attention. Her mind was too busy recounting all the magical dream adventures with Harry and finally seeing her dad after months.

She remembered that her mum had prepared her favourite packed lunch of spinach and cheese börek (a small pastry), with an olive salad on the side – and chocolate cookies for dessert. "Yes!" thought Maya, smiling.

At lunchtime, Maya and Archie sat on a bench in the playground, having eaten in the main hall. "How was your weekend, Maya?" he asked. "I went to see my dad in prison. It was nice, but I hate leaving him, she replied. It's not fair."

"It's not fair!", mimicked Hannah from behind them. Hannah was a girl in Maya's class. She was known for being a bit of a bully. "Moan, moan, moan!", she continued. Maya turned around and told Hannah to shut up. "Why should I? Your dad's in prison because he's a nasty criminal!" shouted Hannah very loudly, so that other children could hear.

Now filled with rage, Maya stood up and pushed Hannah so hard that she fell to the floor.

Hannah didn't waste time getting up and running over to tell her friends. "Just like your dad – a no good troublemaker", she said, as she ran off. Maya felt so angry, she burst into tears. Archie tried to give Maya a hug to comfort her, but she pushed him away. Within minutes, two of Hannah's friends approached Maya and Archie. They looked angry. "Oi, Maya – you better watch out", both girls shouted at her. At this point, Maya's form tutor, Miss Hero, saw them, but was about to ring the bell as lunchtime was over. She told the children that they would talk about what happened, tomorrow. She rang the bell and told the children to get to class.

Maya went home feeling frustrated and sad. She headed straight to her room, as she didn't feel like talking about what happened. Maya was tired of feeling so sad so often. Maya's mum waited a few minutes before going upstairs to check on her. She poured some milk to take to Maya.

Maya was sitting on her bed, drawing in her journal. She sometimes liked to write about how she was feeling – better still, she loved to draw about how she was feeling. Her mum knocked on the door. "Milk delivery!" she called, trying to make Maya laugh. "Thanks, mum", she said. "Can I sit down, sweetheart?" "Ok" replied Maya. Her mum asked what she was drawing. Maya showed her. "They're typhoons – one for each of the rubbish things that has happened", she explained. "One for you and Deniz arguing all the time. One for dad being in prison and one for Hannah being mean to me."

Things I hate!

Mum and her boyfriend Arguing!

Dad in prison!

Being picked on!

Maya's mum praised her for expressing her emotions in ways that were healthy and helpful to her. "Well, I'm hoping we can sort out the first two problems, darling", she said. "But what happened with Hannah?" Maya explained what had happened – her mum was very understanding. "That must have been very upsetting, sweetheart. Well done for defending yourself, but what could you have done instead of pushing Hannah?" "She deserved it – and more", replied Maya. "But hitting people doesn't solve your problems, darling", her mum said. "I should have told Miss Hero?" Maya asked. "Exactly!" her mum replied with a smile. "Let's speak with your teacher about it tomorrow."

Later, Maya went downstairs to join her mum and Deniz for dinner. After dinner, they all watched one of Maya's favourite programmes, before she went up to her room to play on her iPad. She loved playing obbies (that's obstacle course games), especially with Harry cuddled up beside her on the bed.

Harry was having his own fun, chewing on his favourite chew toy.

After a while, Maya's mum came upstairs and told her to get ready for bed. Feeling tired, Maya went to the bathroom to brush her teeth, before giving Harry a kiss and placing him in his cage. As much as Harry loved sleeping beside Maya, nothing could beat the super comfy straw that his bed was made from. He felt safest there – also, there was no chance of Maya kicking him out of the bed!

Maya got into bed and switched her nightlight on. Now that Maya wasn't distracted by her games, she started to think about what happened at school. She could feel her heart starting to beat faster and her breathing getting quicker – just like what happened in the ocean when she saw the trapped sea turtle. Remembering Harry's advice to help calm her down, Maya sat up and took some slow, deep breaths – just as he had shown her – slowly, in through her nose and even more slowly, out through her mouth.

Gradually, she had calmed down enough to try to get some sleep. Maya whispered to herself

"Dreams, come tonight – help make it right!"

Soon after Maya fell asleep, she and Harry found themselves at a spectacular circus!

Maya and Harry were awe-struck as they watched the acrobats swinging from great heights. Hamsters performed terrific tricks, like riding unicycles while juggling and walking a tightwire high above the ground. Some were even jumping through hoops of fire. "This is awesome!" shouted Harry. Maya was so impressed, she couldn't say anything for a few moments!

During the interval, Maya and Harry were lucky enough to go backstage to meet the performers. They were mostly a friendly bunch, but the conversation soon turned unpleasant for Harry, who was being mocked by a few of the other hamsters who had asked him where he lived. "I live with my best friend, Maya", he said, smiling. "I sleep in a cage and –"

Harry didn't even get to finish his sentence because one of the hamsters laughed at him. "HA! In a cage? Did you hear that everyone? So she basically keeps you locked in a prison and you think that's a good life?"

"We have lots of fun together and Maya loves me!" Harry replied. But Maya could see that he was upset. She could tell, as his tiny nose started to twitch ferociously.

Maya felt that familiar fiery fury rise inside her. "STOP". She shouted at the hamsters. "Harry is my best friend and actually – he's no more in a prison than you are! Harry comes out of his cage whenever he wants. Can you?" This made Maya think about her dad – she hated the idea that Harry's life was similar to her dad's in prison.

Suddenly, one of the jugglers spoke. "Come on everyone! Maya and Harry are our guests. We've got so much in common – let's give them a second half they'll never forget!"

He threw Maya a brightly coloured juggling ball. "This is for you. You might need it soon." Maya caught it with one hand and put the precious ball in her bag.

The juggler called the performers to get ready for the second half. Maya and Harry settled back down into their seats to watch the second half of the performance. It had barely started when Maya heard her mum softly saying "good morning". Maya woke up feeling a little sad to leave the circus behind and also anxious about the day ahead. She remembered that she would have to speak with Miss Hero and Hannah about what happened the day before.

She got up and reached into her bag, hoping that she would find a *keeper* that might help the meeting go well. "YES!" exclaimed Maya as she held up the brightly coloured ball. Maya began to feel that warm glow deep inside her again.

"I know!" said Maya to herself . . .

Later that day at school, Miss Hero asked Maya if they could have a brief talk before the meeting. Nervously, Maya agreed and they met after lunch in the library. Miss Hero gave Maya a big smile as she invited her to sit down beside her on one of the sofas (which was empty for a change!). Maya felt the knots in her tummy ease.

Gently mentioning her surprise at Maya pushing Hannah, Miss Hero asked her if she was ok and whether she wanted to tell her anything. Maya felt as if she were about to drown in an overwhelming wave of emotion. She started to cry.

Miss Hero asked if she wanted a hug. Maya couldn't speak for crying so much, but she managed to nod "yes". Maya held on tightly to Miss Hero and gradually, she was able to calm down and explain why she pushed Hannah.

When it was time for the meeting, Maya remembered how she wanted to use the juggling ball and suggested to Miss Hero that they use the juggling ball to help everyone have their turn to speak, without any interruptions. "How will that work?" she asked. Maya explained that whoever is holding the juggling ball can talk, while everyone else has to listen. "That's a great idea, Maya – well done!" said Miss Hero. "I know that we can sort this out." Even Hannah nodded, feeling a little awkward.

Sometimes Maya found it hard to find the right words to express herself (which is why she loved to draw about how she felt in her journal), but while holding the ball, Maya felt strong. She told Hannah that what she had said was cruel and that her dad was a caring person, who had made a mistake and that she missed him all the time. Despite Hannah being mean to her, she did feel bad for pushing her. Remembering what her mum told her – that hitting people doesn't solve her problems – Maya apologised for this. She felt nervous about having to listen to what Hannah had to say, but, remembering her own rules, Maya took a deep breath and felt more prepared to listen to Hannah.

Hannah realised that what she had said to Maya was very unkind. She hadn't really stopped to think about how Maya might feel, being separated from her dad. When she took the ball from Maya, she looked sad and in a quiet voice said "I'm sorry Maya. I was only joking. I guess I'm used to my brothers picking on me, so I didn't think how it would feel for someone else." Maya took the ball and thanked Hannah, feeling bad about what she had done. She asked if she would like to play with her and Archie during lunch break. Hannah excitedly took the ball and quickly replied "yes please!"

"How about a game of football?" As Miss Hero started to speak, Maya, holding the ball, said "No, Miss! You need to have the ball before you speak!" They all laughed!

Miss Hero took the juggling ball and praised them both. "How about this game of football?" she asked. She gave the ball back to Maya to keep safely and waited outside with Hannah while Maya collected her things.

Maya put the *keeper* safely back in her bag. Hannah, feeling excited and impatient, called out "come on, Maya – last one to the playground stinks of rotten eggs!"

Laughing, Maya ran outside, joint first with Hannah – Miss Hero, trailing behind, chuckled – "looks like I stink of rotten eggs, then!"

Later that evening, Maya sat down on her bed, sitting Harry beside her. She knew that her life could be tough – really tough. But when she thought about it, she knew that she was strong and that she had lots of ways to overcome her problems. She noticed that she was feeling more positive than she had in a long time. Wanting to hold on to this feeling, she took her journal. She decided to make a list of all the things in her life that made her feel happy and safe.

Things that make me happy!

1. Mum's hugs
2. Dad
3. Playing football
4. My friends
5. Telling Miss Hero my problems
6. My dream adventures

Maya felt something ticklish on her toes. It was Harry having a nibble at them! "Harry, that's ticklish, stop it! Don't worry – you know I'm going to put you on my list!" She paused to write Harry's name on her list.

7. Harry

8. Taking slow deep breaths

9. Writing and drawing in my diary

10. My Keepers

"That is a looooooooooooong list!" Maya said to Harry. The list helped her to see that the good things in her life far outweighed the bad things that happened.

She felt that warm glow deep inside her.

Maya took a slow deep breath and said

"When things go wrong, I can be strong!"